Explorers & Discoverers

Compiled by Donna Bailey

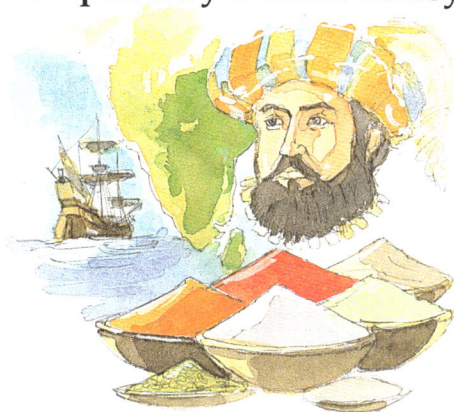

Illustrated by Peter Rutherford

HENDERSON
PUBLISHING PLC

Woodbridge, Suffolk, IP12 1BY England
© 1994 Henderson Publishing plc

AMUNDSEN, *Roald (1872-1928) Norwegian explorer*
Amundsen was the first person to sail through the
North-West Passage from the Atlantic to the Pacific
Ocean, north of Canada. It took him 3 years and he
spent 2 long polar winters while the sea was iced
over. He was also the first person to reach the South
Pole, using sledges hauled by a team of dogs. He
died searching for a friend who was reported
missing in the Arctic.

BAFFIN, *William (c.1584-1622) English navigator*
Baffin tried to discover a route to India by the
North-West Passage, north of Canada. He explored
the Hudson Strait and gave his name to Baffin
Island. He sailed 483 kilometres further than
previous explorers. There seemed no hope of
finding the passage, so he gave up and made
surveys of the Red Sea and the Persian Gulf.

BAKER, *Sir Samuel White (1821-1893)*
English explorer
Baker wanted to discover the source of the Nile
river and spent a year exploring the Nile tributaries
around the borders of Sudan and Ethiopia. Using
maps supplied by Speke, Baker found the source
to be a lake which he named Lake Albert. He later
led a military expedition to help put down the
slave trade.

BARENTS, *Willem (c.1550-1597) Dutch navigator*
Barents tried to find a north-east passage to the Far
East. He rounded northern Europe and sighted
Spitsbergen (now Svalbard), but his ship became
trapped in the ice. Barents and his men were forced
to winter in a shelter built on the Russian island of
Novaya Zemlaya. In June they set out for the
mainland in open boats, but Barents died within a
week. The Barents Sea is named after him.

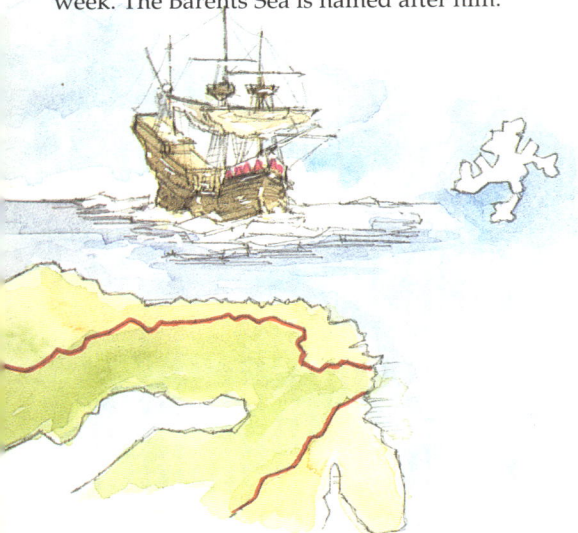

BASS, *George (1771-1803) English sailor*
Bass made an important survey of the eastern coast
of Australia and explored the George's River,
Botany Bay, and the coast south of Sydney. He
studied the animals and plants of the region and
discovered the strait between New South Wales
and Van Diemen's Land (Tasmania), called the Bass
Strait after him. On his last voyage he sailed from
Sydney bound for South America and was never
heard of again.

BEAN, *Alan (1932-) and* **CONRAD,** *Charles (1930-)*
American astronauts
Bean was a member of the Apollo 12 mission to the
Moon in 1969. In spite of being struck by lightening
at take off, Bean and Conrad landed the lunar
module safely on the Moon. They carried out a
number of scientific experiments and made the first
lunar walk, a distance of about 2 kilometres, while
they collected samples of moon rocks.

BERING, *Vitus (1681-1741) Danish navigator*
In 1724 the Tsar of Russia asked Bering to find out
if Asia and north America were connected by land.
Bering sailed through the Bering Strait from the
north Atlantic into the Arctic Ocean and proved
the two continents were not joined up. On a second
voyage he mapped the coast of Alaska and the
Aleutian Islands, but he became ill with scurvy. His
ship was wrecked on Bering Island, where he died.

BIRD, *Isabella (1832-1904) English traveller*
Isabella suffered from a spinal illness and travelled
all over the world seeking a cure. She described the
journeys she made to the USA, Persia, Tibet,
Kurdistan, China, Japan and Korea in her many
books. Her last journey was made in 1901 when
she travelled over 1600 kilometres in Morocco.

BLASHFORD-SNELL, *John (1936-) British explorer*
Blashford-Snell has made many expeditions to
different parts of the world, including the first
descent and exploration of the Blue Nile; a journey
north to south from Alaska to Cape Horn, and the
first complete navigation of the Zaire river in Africa.
He organised the adventure training schemes
Operation Drake and Operation Raleigh to give
young people a taste of adventure.

BLIGH, *William (1754-1817) English admiral*
Bligh commanded HMS Bounty on a voyage from
Tahiti in the South Seas to the West Indies. On the
journey his crew, led by Christian Fletcher, mutinied
and seized the ship. They cast Bligh and 18 men
adrift in a long boat with no weapons or
instruments. Bligh and his men rowed more than
5750 kilometres across the Pacific to Timor, with no
lives lost. Bligh continued his career in the navy,
served under Nelson, and was appointed governor
of New South Wales in Australia.

BLYTH, *Charles (Chay) (1940-) British sailor*
Blyth rowed across the Atlantic with Captain John
Ridgeway in 1966, and sailed solo around the world
in a westerly direction during 1970-71. In 1973-74 he
and a crew sailed in the opposite direction, and in
1977 he made a record-breaking transatlantic
crossing from Cape Verde to Antigua.

BURKE, *Robert O'Hara (1820-1861)*
Australian explorer
Burke led the first expedition to cross Australia from north to south. They reached northern Australia but the jungle scrub blocked their way to the coast. On the return journey Burke and two of his 3 men died of exhaustion.

BURTON, *Sir Richard (1821-1890) British traveller*
Burton learned 40 different languages. He disguised himself as a Muslim trader and travelled the bandit-ridden route from Medina to Mecca. He made an even more dangerous journey to the forbidden city of Harar in eastern Ethiopia, and became the first European to enter the city without losing his life. He rode back across the desert almost without food and water. Burton set out with Speke to find the source of the Nile. They discovered Lake Tanganyika, but Burton became so ill from malaria that he could not walk, and Speke pushed on without him.

CABOT, *John (1450-1498) Venetian navigator*
Cabot settled in England and was sent by Henry VII
to find new lands and colonies for England. His tiny
ship with a crew of 18 sailed west, and after 7 weeks
reached Newfoundland. Cabot thought he had
reached China and on his return to England gave a
favourable report to the King. He made a second
voyage to the coast of Greenland, sailed down to
Labrador and finally returned to Bristol where he
died later that year.

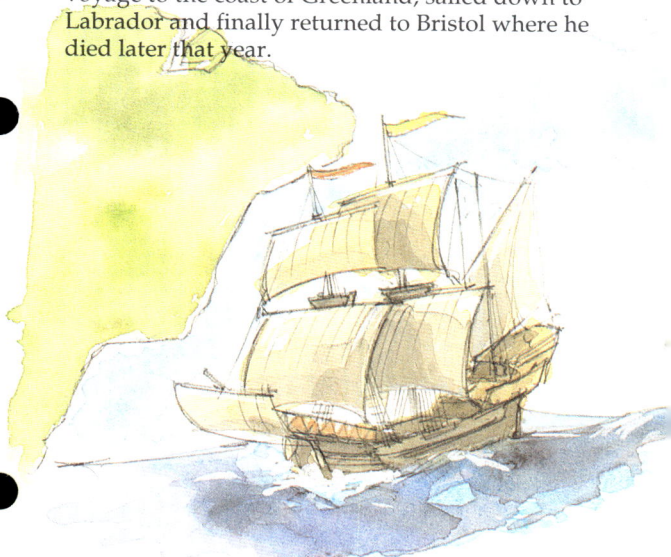

CABRAL, *Pedro Alvarez (1460-1526)*
Portuguese navigator
When Vasco da Gama returned from his voyage to
India, the King of Portugal sent Cabral with 13 ships
to trade in the East. Cabral accidentally reached
Brazil by taking a course too far to the west. He
claimed the country for Portugal, then continued
his journey around the Cape of Good Hope to
Calcutta in India where he set up a Portuguese
trading station.

CARTER, *Howard (1873-1939) British archaeologist*
Carter was working in Egypt when he made the
famous discovery of the tomb of Tutankhamen. It
took him 3 days to uncover the sealed entrance to
the tomb and 10 years to supervise the removal of
its treasures to the Cairo Museum.

CARTIER, *Jacques (1491-1557) French explorer*
Cartier was sent by the French King to search for
gold. He sailed westwards and explored the coast
of Newfoundland then sailed up the Gulf of
St Lawrence and landed at Cape Gaspe, taking
possession of the land for France. On his next
expedition he discovered the St Lawrence River and
sailed upstream to the place where Quebec now
stands. From there he set off in the smallest of his
ships to explore further, finally reaching an Indian
village later named Montreal.

CAVENDISH, *Thomas (1555-1592) English navigator*
Cavendish was the leader of the third expedition to sail around the world. He sailed from Plymouth to Brazil and down the coast to Patagonia. After passing through the Straits of Magellan, he attacked Spanish shipping before he sailed to the Philippines, rounded the Cape of Good Hope to St Helena, and reached Plymouth after 2 years and 50 days.

CHANCELLOR, *Richard (d.1556) English navigator*
Chancellor led 3 ships to find the north-east passage from England to China, but the other 2 ships in the expedition were lost in a storm. Chancellor continued on into the White Sea, then journeyed overland to Moscow, where he was warmly welcomed by the Tsar. He returned to England with a trade agreement between Russia and England.

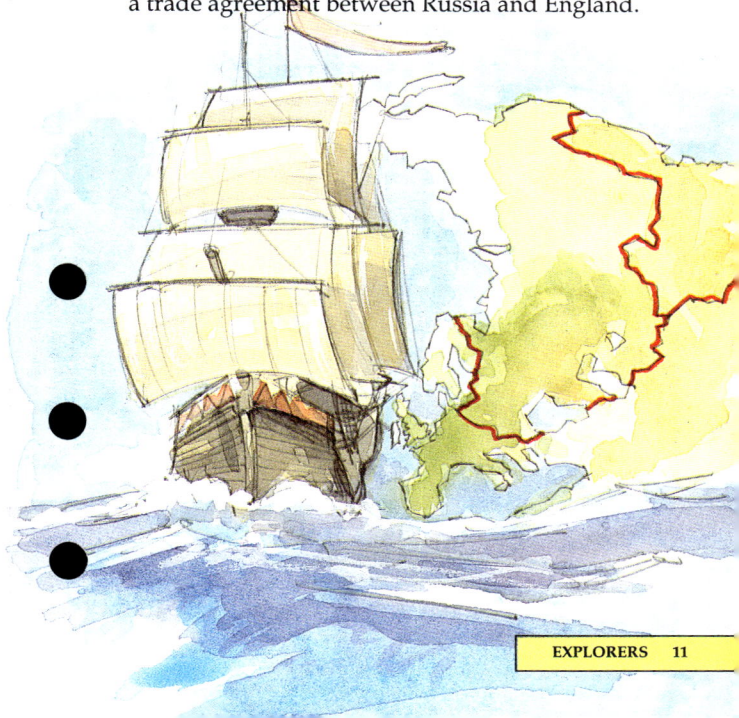

CLAPPERTON, *Hugh (1788-1827) English explorer*
Clapperton joined a British expedition that
journeyed southwards from Tripoli across the
Sahara. He discovered Lake Chad and travelled
widely in northern Nigeria. On a later expedition he
crossed the Niger River, and travelled from Kano to
Sokoto where he died.

COLUMBUS, *Christopher (1451-1506)*
Italian born navigator
Columbus hoped that if he sailed west he would
reach Japan. He persuaded the Spanish King to give
him the money for 3 small ships and after leaving
the Canaries he sailed west for 3 weeks. His crew
were terrified they would fall off the edge of the
world but Columbus calmed their fears and they
soon sighted land. Columbus thought he had
reached India, but in fact he had arrived at the
Bahamas. He cruised around the islands and on his
return to Spain was hailed as a hero. Columbus
made several more journeys to the West Indies, and
touched the mainlands of both Central America and
South America. After troubles with his men and the
Indians he returned to
Spain where he
died in poverty,
still believing
that he had
reached the
Orient.

CONRAD, *Charles (1930-) American astronaut*
Conrad was co-pilot of the Gemini 11 spacecraft and commanded the Apollo 12 flight to the Moon. The team spent a total of 31 hours on the Moon before successfully returning to Earth. Conrad also commanded the Skylab mission and docked their Apollo spacecraft with the orbiting Skylab. They managed to repair the Skylab which had been damaged during its launch.

COOK, *James (1728-1779) English navigator*
Cook was a skilled navigator who charted the St Lawrence River in Canada, the coast of New Zealand and the eastern coast of Australia, where he discovered Botany Bay. He returned to England via the East Indies and the Cape of Good Hope, a journey of 3 years. On his last journey he discovered Hawaii, where he was murdered during a scuffle on shore.

CORTÉS, *Hernan (1485-1547) Spanish adventurer*
Cortés went to the West Indies in search of
adventure. The Spanish governor of Cuba sent him
to explore the Mexican mainland with a small force.
He met the Aztec ruler Montezuma who gave him a
friendly welcome. Montezuma was killed during a
riot and Cortés and his followers had to escape.
Cortés returned and destroyed their capital city and
killed thousands of Aztecs. He ruled Mexico as
governor for 9 years, but Charles V of Spain grew
so jealous of his power that he ordered Cortés back
to Spain.

COUSTEAU, *Jacques (1910-) French oceanographer*
Cousteau was interested in underwater exploration
and helped invent the aqualung, which allows
divers to breathe under water. He developed the
first underwater diving station and an observation
vessel called a diving saucer. He took amazing
underwater photographs from these vessels.
Cousteau did much to prevent the pollution of
the sea bed by the dumping of nuclear waste.

DAMPIER, *William (1652-1715) English explorer*
Dampier spent 10 years as a pirate, raiding the coast of Peru, Mexico and Chile. He was sent to explore round Australia and the Pacific islands. Dampier landed in north Australia and some off-shore islands are named after him. During his 3 year voyage around the world he found Alexander Selkirk, a Scottish sailor, marooned on an uninhabited island in the Pacific, on whose adventures Daniel Defoe based his story of Robinson Crusoe.

DAVIS, *John (1550-11605) English navigator*
Davis discovered the Falkland Islands on a voyage to find a passage through the Straits of Magellan. On a later voyage to the East Indies he was killed by Japanese pirates.

DEZHNYOV, *Semyon (c.1605-1673) Russian explorer*
Dezhnyov travelled in the north of Siberia and
sailed eastward from the Kolyma River towards the
Bering Strait. He was the first European to sail
through the Bering Strait and prove that Asia and
North America were separate, but his report lay
hidden for a hundred years.

DIAZ, *Bartholomeu (c.1459-1500) Portuguese navigator*
King John of Portugal sent Diaz on an expedition to
look for a sea route to India around Africa. Diaz
sailed south with 3 ships and landed near Angra
Pequena (now Luderitz Bay) to claim the land for
Portugal. He was then caught in a storm and was
driven from sight of land. When the storm ended,
Diaz turned east then north, and reached Mossel
Bay on the south coast of Africa. After sailing east
for 3 more days, he saw that the African coast
turned northwards and the way to India was clear,
but his crew insisted on going home. Diaz was the
first European to round the southern tip of Africa,
which he called the Cape of Storms, but which King
John renamed the Cape of Good Hope.

DRAKE, *Sir Francis (c.1540-1596) English sailor*
Drake helped Hawkins in the slave trade between West Africa and America. A surprise attack by Spanish ships in the West Indies made Drake a life-long enemy of Spain. He returned several times to the West Indies to plunder and attack Spanish ships. King Philip of Spain planned to send a fleet to punish the English, but Drake raided the harbour at Cadiz and burned the fleet. The Spanish equipped a new fleet, an armada of 130 ships. Drake helped defeat the Armada, and died at sea 7 years later during another raid on the Spanish colonies in America.

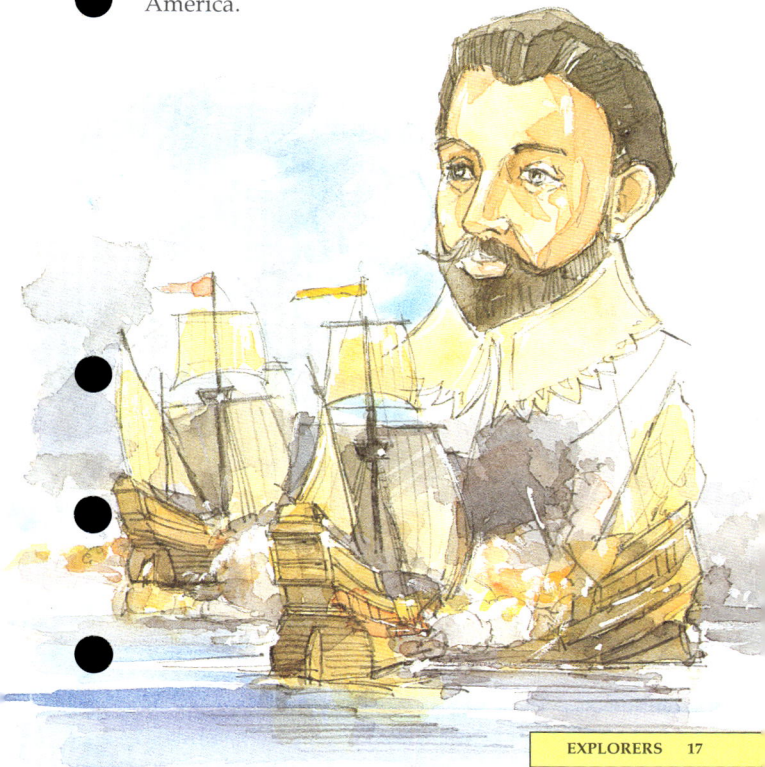

E

ERIC THE RED, *(late 10th century) Viking explorer*
Eric was a Viking who discovered and named
Greenland. Eric settled in Iceland with his family
but after a quarrel with other Icelanders, was forced
to leave. He sailed
westward and
arrived at the
coast of
Greenland
where he
spent 3 years
hunting and
fishing.

ERIKSSON, *Leif (11th century) Viking explorer*
Leif Eriksson was the son of Eric the Red. The
Norwegian King Olaf Trygvesson sent Leif to
convert the Icelanders to Christianity. Leif set out
westwards, but was blown off course. After many
weeks he came to a fertile land full of vines
(probably Nova Scotia in Canada), which he
called Vinland. Leif was the first European to
discover America.

FIENNES, *Celia (1662-1741) English traveller*
Celia was a well-off Puritan lady who travelled about 3000 miles on horseback throughout England. She visited places like Nottingham, Leeds, Norwich, Liverpool and Ipswich. Her journal describes her travels and tells us a lot about the life of the countryside in the later Stuart period.

FIENNES, *Ranulph (1944-) English explorer*
Fiennes made the first surface journey around the world's polar axis. His earlier expeditions included an exploration of the White Nile, of the Jostedalsbre Glacier (Norway) and the Headless Valley (Canada). He was forced by exhaustion to give up his latest attempt to walk to the South Pole on foot .

FLINDERS, *Matthew (1774-1814) Australian explorer*
Flinders explored and charted with Bass the south-east coast of Australia in a boat called Tom Thumb, which was only 2.5 metres long. On another journey he sailed all the way around Australia and mapped the whole of the east, south and most of the north coasts.

FRANKLIN, *Sir John (1786-1847) British explorer*
Franklin led an overland canoe expedition from the
western shore of Hudson Bay to the Arctic Ocean.
He then explored, still by canoe, 880 kilometres of
the coast of northern Canada. He later explored the
north-west American coast from the mouth of the
Mackenzie River. Franklin wanted to discover the
North-West passage connecting the Atlantic and
Pacific Oceans north of Canada. He set out with 2
ships, but the expedition was lost. Twelve years
later the skeletons of the ships' crews were found on
King William Island, together with a diary
describing the journey. The ships had been frozen
and crushed by the ice in Victoria Strait.

FUCHS, *Sir Vivian (1909-) English explorer*
Fuchs accompanied several expeditions to
Greenland, Africa (where he surveyed the Rift
Valley in the Ethiopia-Kenya area) and to
Antarctica. He led the 12-man Commonwealth
Transantarctic Expedition which completed the first
land journey across Antarctica and proved that a
single continent exists beneath the Antarctic polar
ice sheet.

GAMA, *Vasco da (c.1460-1524) Portuguese navigator*
The King of Portugal asked Da Gama to find a sea
route to India round the Cape of Good Hope.
Da Gama set sail with 4 small ships and reached the
Cape after 3 months without seeing land. He cruised
north up the African coast as far as Malindi, and an
Arab pilot guided them to India where they landed
at Calcutta. Da Gama returned to Portugal with his
ship laden with spices, and the king rewarded him
with wealth and honours. Da Gama made 2 more
voyages to India and set up new trading stations
along the Indian coast.

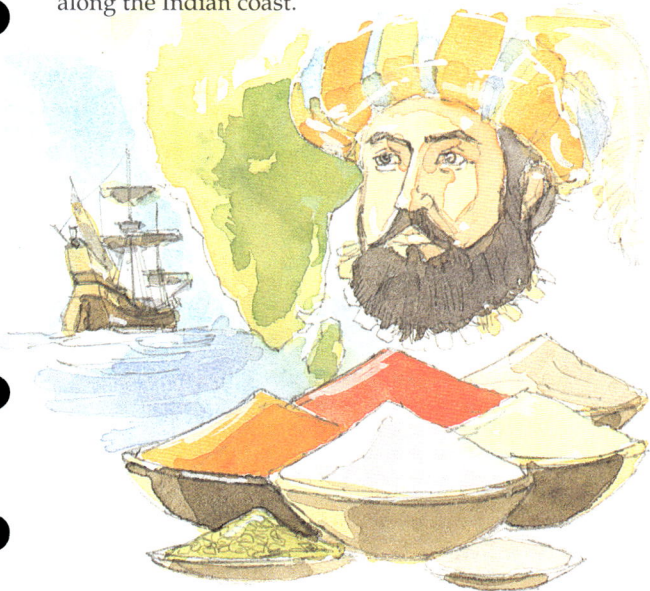

GILBERT, *Sir Humphrey (c.1540-1583) English sailor*
Gilbert led an expedition to North America to found
an English colony at St John's, Newfoundland. On
his return journey his ship was sunk in a storm and
all on board were drowned.

HAWKINS, *Sir John (1532-1595) English sailor*
Hawkins made his fortune by taking part in the slave trade carrying slaves from West Africa to the West Indies. He became treasurer to the Navy and used his experience of ships to improve the design of the ships in the navy. He commanded one of the ships that defeated the Armada, then went with Drake on a raid to the Spanish West Indies. He died off Puerto Rico and was buried at sea.

HEARNE, *Samuel (1745-1792) English explorer*
Hearne was the first European to make the overland trip from Hudson's Bay to Coppermine, which he named, in the far north of Canada. He walked some 5,000 miles with only an Indian guide and the guide's 8 wives. He later built a trading post on the Saskatchewan River to trade in furs. When the French plundered and destroyed the post, Hearne was taken prisoner. The French commander encouraged Hearne to write an account of his historic journey in the Arctic.

HEDIN, *Sven (1865-1952) Swedish explorer*
Hedin led a series of expeditions through Central
Asia and made several important archaeological and
geographical findings. He explored routes across the
Himalayas and produced the first maps of Tibet. He
travelled with a Sino-Swedish expedition across the
Gobi desert, and discovered important Stone Age
remains on the China-Mongolia border.

HENRY the Navigator, *Prince (1394-1460)*
Portuguese prince
Henry was not an explorer himself but spent his life
financing and encouraging voyages of exploration.
He set up a college of navigation and employed the
best geographers, map-makers, astronomers and
boat builders he could find. He sent expeditions
further and further south along the African coast.
His sailors discovered the Madeira Islands, the Cape
Verde Islands and sailed as far as Sierra Leone in
West Africa.

HERBERT, *Wally (1934-) English explorer*
Herbert made the first crossing by dog sledge of
the Arctic Ocean, from Alaska to Spitsbergen via the
North Pole. His journey of 6000 kilometres was the
longest continuous sledge journey in polar
exploration.

HEYERDAHL, *Thor (1914-) Norwegian explorer*
Heyerdahl proved that ancient civilisations could
make long ocean voyages. On his first journey in the
Kon Tiki he sailed from Peru in South America to
Eastern Polynesia. He then built the *Ra*, a replica of
an ancient Egyptian reed boat, which he sailed
across the Atlantic from Morocco to the Caribbean.
On another voyage in the *Tigris*, a replica of an
ancient Sumerian craft, he sailed from Iraq to
Djibouti in the Gulf of Aden.

HILLARY, *Sir Edmund (1919-) New Zealand explorer*
Hillary was a member of the British Everest
expedition in 1953. Hillary and his Sherpa guide
Tenzing Norgay made the final climb to the
summit of Everest, 8,848 metres high, the
first people to climb the world's
highest mountain. Hillary later
led the New Zealand group,
part of the Common-
wealth Transantarctic
expedition, to the
South Pole
travelling
on a tractor.

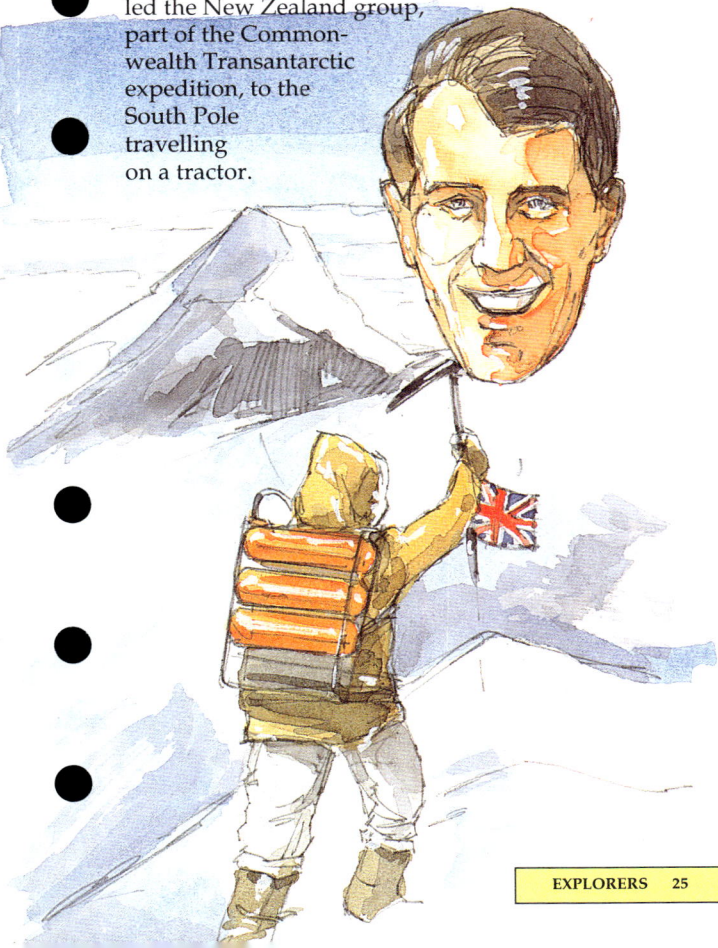

H

HUDSON, Henry (c.1550-1611) *English explorer*
Hudson wanted to find a sea route to the Far East.
He sailed east and followed the coast of Greenland
but found thick ice barring his way. On a second
journey he sailed north-east beyond Norway but
was again blocked by ice. On his third journey he
sailed west to North America and up the coast
searching for a channel leading westwards. He
found New York harbour and sailed up the Hudson
River, claiming the land for Holland. On his last
voyage he set sail in the Discovery in search of
a north-west passage to China. He
discovered Hudson Bay, where his ship
was frozen fast in the ice during the
winter and the food ran short. In
the spring his crew mutinied
and set Hudson, his son
and 7 others adrift in a
small boat. They were
never seen again.

HUMBOLDT, *Alexander von (1769-1859)*
German explorer
Humboldt and a companion spent 5 years exploring
the rainforests surrounding the Amazon and the
Orinoco Rivers in South America. In Peru he
measured the temperature of the Atlantic Ocean
and charted the oceans' currents, today called the
Humboldt currents. He later spent 6 months in
Siberia studying its weather and geology and
organised the setting up of a chain of weather
stations around the world.

IBN BATTUTA, *(1304-1378) Arab traveller*
Ibn Battuta went on an extraordinary 120,000 kilometre journey that took 30 years. He set out from his home in Tangier in Morocco on a pilgrimage to Mecca via Tunis and Damascus. He travelled in Asia Minor (now Turkey), north to Russia, and east to India and China. On his return he visited Spain and travelled across the Sahara to Timbuktu.

IRWIN, *James (1930-1991) American astronaut*
Irwin piloted the lunar module during the Apollo 15 mission. He walked on the Moon and made 3 separate excursions with mission commander David Scott in the Lunar Rover. They drove nearly 28 kilometres across the Moon's surface to collect samples of rocks and conduct scientific experiments. They stayed nearly 3 days on the Moon before they rejoined the command module and returned to Earth.

JOLLIET, *Louis (1645-1700) French Canadian explorer*
Jolliet explored and made maps of much of the unknown wilderness of the Great Lakes and the Mississippi River. He paddled in a canoe up the St Lawrence river, through the Great Lakes and down Lake Michigan. He was the first European to travel down the Mississippi between Illinois and the Arkansas. He later explored Hudson Bay, the Gulf of St Lawrence and the coast of Labrador.

KINGSLEY, *Mary (1862-1900) British explorer*
Kingsley decided at the age of 30 to go to Africa to study African religion and law. She was the first European to enter Gabon, and explored the forests north of the river Zaire on foot and by paddling a dug-out canoe. On her return to England she wrote 2 successful books about her adventures. She died in South Africa while nursing sick prisoners during the Boer War.

LANDER, *Richard, (1804-1834) English explorer*
Lander explored West Africa and traced the course
of the lower Niger River to its delta where he was
seized by the local inhabitants and held captive until
a large ransom was paid. On a later trading
expedition up the Niger, Lander was wounded by
tribesmen attacking his canoe, and died soon after.

LA SALLE, *Robert (1643-1687) French explorer*
La Salle dreamed of building a French empire
around the fur trade in North America. He crossed
the Great Lakes and explored the area around Lake
Michigan. He was the first European to travel down
the Mississippi to the Gulf of Mexico. He claimed
the lands around the mouth of the Mississippi for
France and founded Louisiana. He returned with
some colonists to found a settlement, but failed to
find the mouth of the Mississippi again. His men
turned against him and murdered him.

LEWIS, *Meriwether (1774-1809) American explorer*
Lewis and William Clark were chosen by President
Jefferson to explore the lands from the Mississippi
River to the Pacific coast. They sailed up the
Mississippi and spent the winter in North Dakota.
In the spring they continued up the Missouri River
until it became too narrow for the boats to pass. The
Indians helped them cross the Rocky Mountains to
the Columbia River, and several weeks later they
reached the Pacific.

LIVINGSTONE, *David (1813-1873) Scottish explorer*
On one of his early missionary journeys in Africa he
was attacked by a lion and nearly lost an arm. He
decided that it was his duty to explore the unknown
centre of Africa. On his first expedition he walked
from the middle of Africa to the Atlantic coast, then
turned around and headed east until he reached the
Indian ocean, becoming the first European to see the
Victoria Falls.
Livingstone discovered Lake Nyasa, but
disappeared on another expedition to find the
source of the Nile. He was discovered, worn out
and almost starving,
by Stanley on the
shores of Lake
Tanganyika,
who met him
with the
famous words
"Dr Livingstone,
I presume."

MACKENZIE, *Alexander (1755-1820)*
Scottish explorer
Mackenzie was a fur trader who set up a trading post on Lake Athabasca. He was the first European to follow the Mackenzie River, named after him, by canoe from the Great Slave Lake to the river's delta on the Arctic Ocean. He was also the first to cross the Rocky Mountains to the Pacific.

MAGELLAN, *Ferdinand (1480-1521)*
Portuguese navigator
Magellan thought there must be a way around the Americas to the East Indies. He offered his services to the King of Spain and set out with 5 ships and succeeded in getting 3 of them to the eastern entrance of the strait named after him at the bottom of South America. It took 38 days to battle through the Magellan Strait to the Pacific Ocean. Magellan was later killed in a fight with the natives in the Philippines, but one of his ships sailed on and completed the first circumnavigation of the world, proving that the Earth was round.

MORGAN, *Sir Henry (c.1635-1688) Welsh adventurer*
Morgan was a pirate who attacked many Spanish ships and coastal towns in the West Indies and South America. His greatest adventure was a dash from the Caribbean Sea across the narrow jungle-clad strip of Panama to the Pacific coast to capture Panama City. Morgan burned the city to the ground and looted its treasures. He needed 175 mules to carry all the treasure away. King Charles made him governor of Jamaica where he hunted down both English and Spanish pirates!

NANSEN, *Fridtjof (1861-1930) Norwegian explorer*
Nansen started his travels by crossing Greenland on
skis. Then he noticed the movement of driftwood
across the Arctic Ocean and decided to try and drift to
the North Pole. He built a special ship that would not
be crushed in the ice and sailed along the Arctic coast
of Russia, allowing the ship to get frozen in. When he
saw it would not pass right over the North Pole he set
out with a companion on skis and reached within 400
kilometres of the Pole.

NORDENSKIÖLD, *N. Adolf (1832-1901)*
Swedish explorer
Nordenskiöld led several expeditions to Greenland
to study the inland ice. He was the first person to
discover the North-East Passage. He sailed round the
north of Russia to Siberia where the ship was caught
in the ice for over 9 months.

OATES, *Laurence (1880-1912) British explorer*
Oates was a member of Scott's second expedition to the South Pole. On the return journey, suffering from frostbite, he went out alone into the blizzard to die rather than delay the others.

ORELLANA, *Francisco de (c.1490-c.1546)*
Spanish explorer
Orellana helped Pizzaro during the conquest of Peru. He was sent with Pizzaro's half brother Gonzalo to explore the unknown regions east of Quito, but went on ahead and left Gonzalo behind. Orellana was the first person to navigate the length of the Amazon River from the Napo River to the Atlantic Ocean.

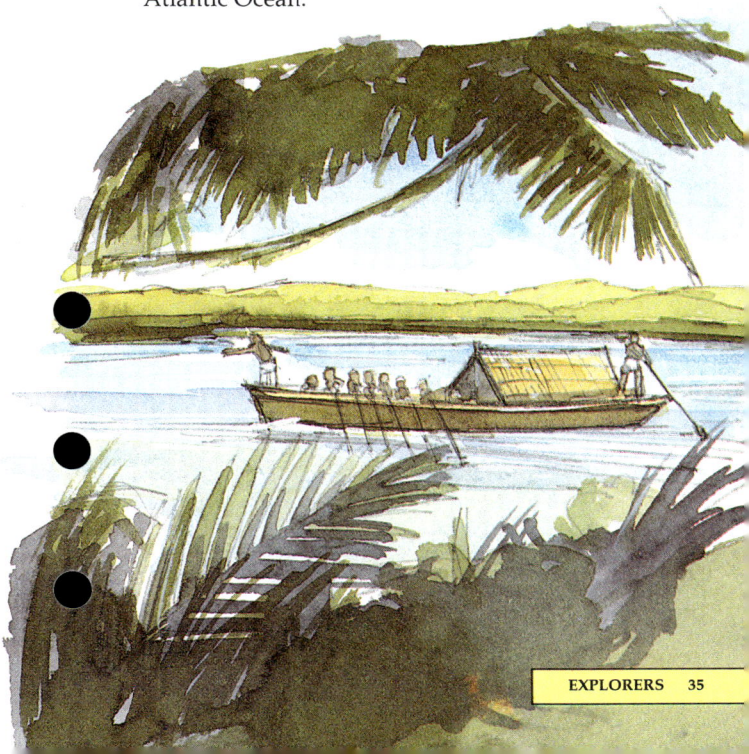

PARK, *Mungo (1771-1806) Scottish explorer*
Park went to Africa to discover the course of the
Niger River. He set out on foot from the mouth of
the River Gambia and travelled inland. He was
captured by some Muslim chiefs and imprisoned,
but managed to escape. Park reached the Niger and
proved that it flowed eastward but had to turn back.
He led another expedition to the Niger, but most
of his companions died of disease and hardship.
Park and 4 others got as far as Bussa in Nigeria,
but their boat was attacked and Park was last seen
jumping overboard.

PEARY, *Robert (1856-1920) American explorer*
Peary decided to be a polar explorer after a trip to Greenland. He led 5 expeditions to Greenland before he set out to reach the North Pole. On the last stage of the journey to the Pole he was accompanied by his black American friend Matthew Henson and 4 Inuit (local eskimo people).
Peary proved Greenland was an island and collected information about the polar seas, tides and winds. He proved that the North Pole is in the centre of a sea covered with ice.

PIZZARO, *Francisco (1470-1541) Spanish adventurer*
Pizzaro heard rumours of the Inca empire in Peru and of its fabulous wealth. After an initial expedition to check it really existed, he returned with 180 men, attacked the capital city and seized the emperor Atahualpa. Pizzaro promised to release him if he would fill a room full of gold and silver. Although this was done, Pizzaro still had Atahualpa put to death, and the Inca resistance collapsed. Pizzaro spread Spanish rule over the Inca empire.

POLO, *Marco (1254-1324) Italian explorer*
Polo's father and uncle invited Marco to go with
them on a trading expedition to China. Their
journey took them overland along the Silk Road,
a route used by silk merchants from China. The
emperor Kublai Khan welcomed them on arrival,
and Marco became a court attendant and travelling
diplomat. His duties took him all over China, to
Siberia, Zanzibar, Burma, Indochina and possibly to
India. The Poly family returned to Venice 20 years
later with marvellous tales about the
things they had seen.

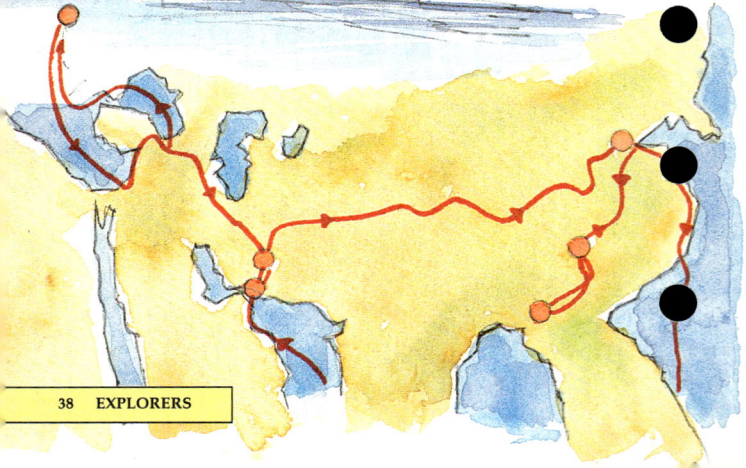

RALEIGH, *Sir Walter (1554-1618) English adventurer*
Raleigh was fascinated by the riches of America and
tried to start a colony at Roanoke, without success.
The members of the expedition brought back
potatoes and tobacco from America and pipe-
smoking became fashionable at court. Inspired by
stories of gold in South America, Raleigh went on
an unsuccessful search for El Dorado.
When Queen Elizabeth died, Raleigh was accused
of treason and imprisoned in the Tower for 13 years.
He persuaded King James to send him on another
search for gold in South America, but was again
unsuccessful. He got into a fight with the Spanish
against the king's orders, and on his return
was beheaded.

ROSS, *James Clark (1800-1862) British explorer*
Ross carried out important surveys of the
magnetism of the North and South Poles. He
discovered the Ross Sea, named after him, and the
Victoria Land region of Antarctica. He charted part
of the coast of Graham Land and sailed around the
Weddell Sea ice.

SCOTT, *Robert Falcon (1868-1912) British explorer*
Scott led 2 expeditions to the Antarctic. On the first
journey, Scott with 2 companions crossed the great
ice barrier and went further south than anyone
before them. His second expedition to the Antarctic
was dogged by ill luck.

Scott and 4 companions set out on the final stretch
and reached the South Pole, only to find Amundsen
had beaten them by a month. On their return
journey they were overtaken by blizzards and all
died from starvation and exposure. Their bodies
were found the following spring together with
Scott's diaries and letters.

SHACKLETON, *Sir Ernest (1874-1922) Irish explorer*
Shackleton joined Scott's first expedition to
Antarctica, but suffered so seriously from scurvy
he had to return home. He decided to lead an
expedition himself and got within 156 kilometres
of the South Pole before shortage of food made him
turn back. On his next attempt, to cross Antarctica
from one side to the other, his ship got trapped in
the ice, was crushed and sank. Shackleton saved his
men and the boats, and they spent 5 months on an
ice floe until they could launch the boats and reach
the barren Elephant Island. From there Shackleton
and 5 others set out in a 6.6 metre boat to get help
from South Georgia, 1290 kilometres away. They
landed on the wrong side of the island but
struggled across the glaciers to Stromness, and
sent a steamer to rescue the rest of the party.

SHEPARD, *Alan (1923-) American astronaut*
Shepard was the first American astronaut to travel
in space in Freedom 7, which reached an altitude
of 185 kilometres. Shepard commanded the Apollo 14
flight which involved the first landing in the lunar
highlands.

SPEKE, *John Hanning (1827-1864) English explorer*
Speke joined Burton on a dangerous expedition to
Somaliland, and 3 years later they went together in
search of the source of the river Nile. They were the
first Europeans to reach Lake Tanganyika. On the
return journey Speke left Burton and struck out on
his own. He discovered Lake Victoria and found the
Nile's exit from the lake, which he named the
Rippon Falls. Back in England Burton and others
challenged his findings. Speke wanted to debate the
subject publicly, but was
killed in a hunting
accident a few hours
before he was due
to appear.

STANLEY, *Sir Henry Morton (1841-1904)
Welsh-American explorer*
Stanley worked as a reporter in Asia Minor (now
Turkey), Crete, Spain and Abyssinia until he was
commissioned by the *New York Herald* to lead an
expedition to find Livingstone. After his success in
doing this, he continued to explore the rivers of
central Africa.

STEFANSSON, *Vihjalmur (1879-1962)*
Icelandic explorer

Stefansson lived for 18 months with the Inuit and learned to speak their language, eat, hunt and fish like them. In an expedition to the Coppermine River and Victoria Island in northern Canada, he proved that it was possible to travel light and live off the country. On another expedition he travelled 960 kilometres over the sea ice, living on seals and polar bears, and mapped a huge area of unknown polar territory.

STUART, *John McDougall (1815-1866)*
Australian explorer
Stuart made a number of expeditions into the
unknown centre of Australia, reaching as far as the
Lake Eyre area. He tried to cross the continent from
south to north, planting the Union Jack in the centre
of Australia on top of Mount Stuart, but was forced
to abandon further exploration northwards because
of lack of water, attacks by aborigines and
scurvy. On another expedition he
succeeded in reaching the north
coast in spite of water
shortages and dense
bushland.

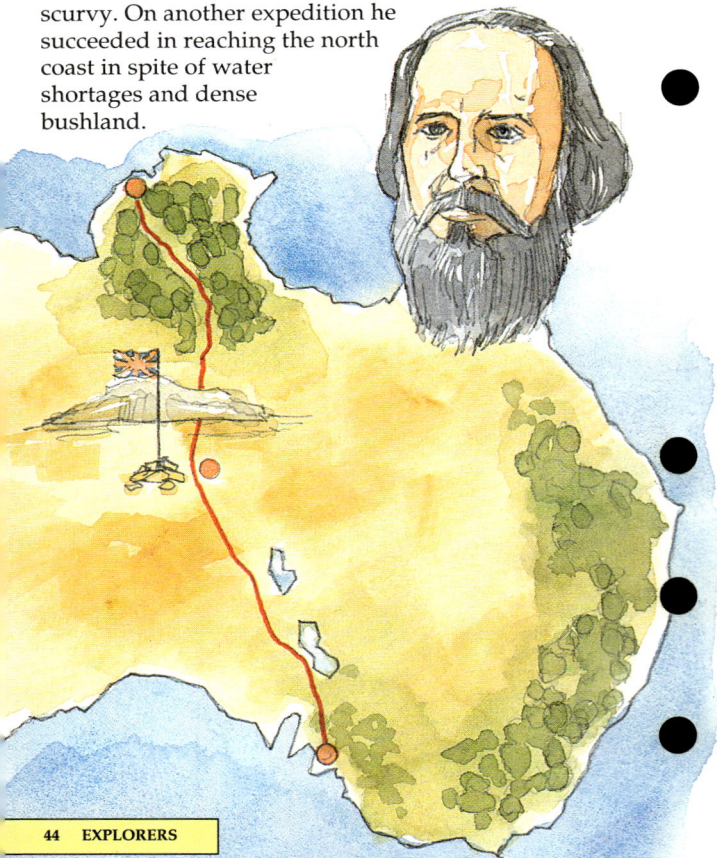

STURT, *Charles (1795-1869) Australian explorer*
Sturt discovered the Darling River and on another
expedition sailed down the Murrumbidgee River
in south-east Australia to the estuary of the Murray
River. Sturt charted the whole river system of the
region. His journey helped to open up vast new
areas for settlement in New South Wales and South
Australia. Sturt led another expedition into the
barren Simpson desert. Sturt was the first to
penetrate central Australia.

T

TASMAN, *Abel (1603-1659) Dutch explorer*
Tasman was sent by Van Diemen, the governor of
the Dutch East Indies, to explore the seas to the
south in the hope of finding a route across the
Pacific to Chile. Tasman sailed west across the
Indian Ocean to Mauritius, then turned south as far
as he dared.

His ships were driven east by the wind until land
was sighted. He called this Van Diemen's Land
(now renamed Tasmania after its discoverer). He
sailed back to Java via Tonga and Fiji, having sailed
all the way around Australia without knowing it.
On a later voyage, Tasman mapped most of the
northern Australian coastline.

TERESHKOVA, *Valentina (1937-) Russian astronaut*
Tereshkova was the first woman to fly in space. She
made a 3 day flight in *Vostok 6*, orbiting the earth
48 times.

VANCOUVER, *George (1757-1798) English navigator*
Vancouver accompanied Cook on 2 journeys, then surveyed parts of Australia, New Zealand, Tahiti and Hawaii. He sailed on to the northwest coast of North America where he made a careful examination of the coast, surveying the inlets and channels near Vancouver Island.

VESPUCCI, *Amerigo (1451-1512) Italian explorer*
Vespucci claimed that he was the first European to reach the mainland of South America. He explored the mouth of the Amazon River and the coast as far south as Río de la Plata, when he realised he was looking at another continent. His information was used by a German map maker who drew the first maps of the New World, and used the name America after Amerigo Vespucci, for the new continent.

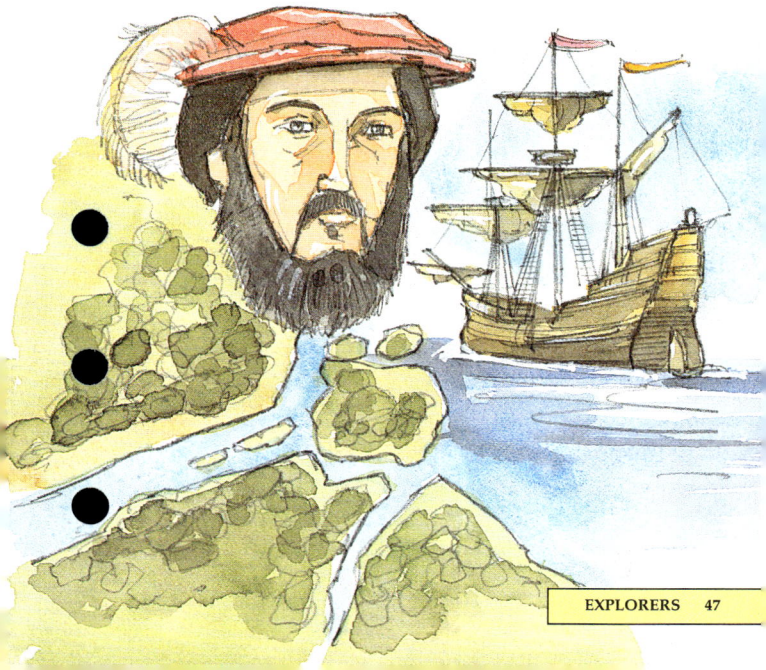

WILKES, *Charles (1798-1877) American navigator*
Wilkes commanded an expedition to the Antarctic
and discovered Wilkes Land, named after him. He
visited islands in the Pacific, explored the west coast
of the United States, then recrossed the Pacific and
returned to New York after sailing round the world.

WILKINS, *Sir George (1888-1958) Australian explorer*
Wilkins pioneered the use of submarines and
aircraft for polar exploration. He flew from Barrow
in Alaska to Green Harbour (Spitsbergen) a journey
lasting twenty and a half hours over unknown
territory. He proved on an Antarctic flight that
Graham Land is an island.